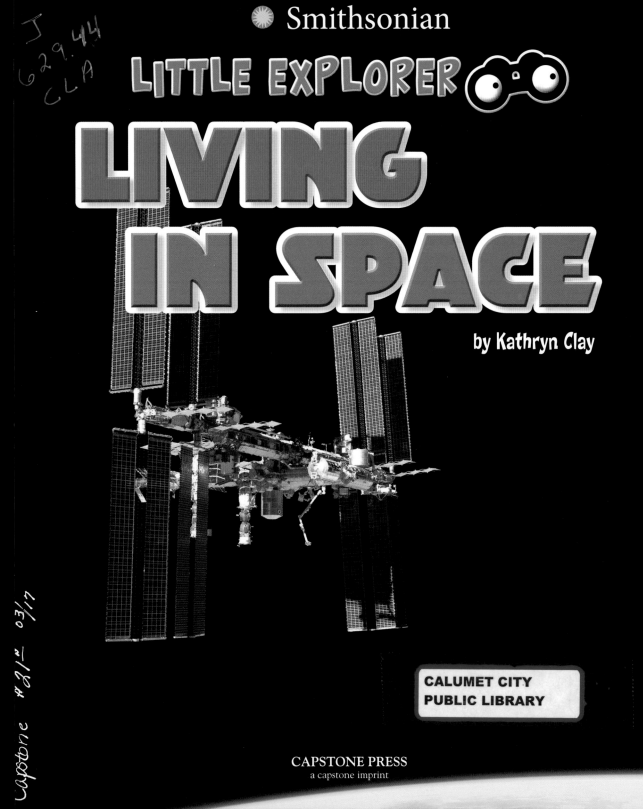

● Smithsonian

LITTLE EXPLORER

LIVING IN SPACE

by Kathryn Clay

CAPSTONE PRESS
a capstone imprint

Little Explorer is published by Capstone Press,
1710 Roe Crest Drive, North Mankato, Minnesota 56003

www.mycapstone.com

Library of Congress Cataloging-in-Publication Data
Names: Clay, Kathryn, author.
Title: Living in space / by Kathryn Clay.
Description: North Mankato, Minnesota : Capstone Press, [2017]
| Series: Smithsonian little explorer. Little astronauts | Audience:
Ages 7–9. | Audience: K to grade 3. | Includes bibliographical
references and index.
Identifiers: LCCN 2016043031 | ISBN 9781515736578 (library
binding) | ISBN 9781515736714 (pbk.) | ISBN 9781515736752
(ebook (pdf))
Subjects: LCSH: International Space Station—Juvenile literature.
| Space Stations—Juvenile literature. | Space environment—
Juvenile literature. | Life support systems (Space environment)—
Juvenile literature. | Outer Space—Exploration—Juvenile
literature.
Classification: LCC TL797.15 .C53 2017 | DDC 629.44/2—dc23
LC record available at https://lccn.loc.gov/2016043031

Editorial Credits
Arnold Ringstad, editor; Laura Polzin, designer and production
specialist

Our very special thanks to Dr. Valerie Neal, Curator and Chair
of the Space History Department at the Smithsonian National
Air and Space Museum for her curatorial review. Capstone
would also like to thank Kealy Gordon, Smithsonian Institution
Product Development Manager, and the following at Smithsonian
Enterprises: Christopher A. Liedel, President; Carol LeBlanc,
Senior Vice President; Brigid Ferraro, Vice President; Ellen
Nanney, Licensing Manager.

Photo Credits
DK Images: Chris Taylor, 13 (top); ESA: NASA, 9; Getty Images:
UIG/Sovfoto, 6, 7 (top); NASA: cover, 1, 2–3, 4 (bottom), 7
(bottom), 8 (foreground), 11, 14, 15, 16, 17 (left), 18, 19, 20, 21, 22,
23 (top), 23 (middle), 23 (bottom), 24, 25 (top left), 25 (bottom
left), 25 (bottom right), 26, 27, Bill Ingalls, 28–29, Carla Cioffi,
12, ESA and the Hubble Heritage Team (STScl/AURA), 29
(inset), Jeff Schmaltz, LANCE MODIS Rapid Response, 25 (top
right), Robert Markowitz, 4 (top), 10; Red Line Editorial: 13, 17
(right); Shutterstock: Julia Kopacheva, 5, pio3, 30–31; Thinkstock:
Stocktrek Images, 13 (bottom)

Design Elements: Shutterstock Images: MarcelClemens;
Ovchinnkov Vladimir; pio3; Shay Yacobinski; Tashal; Teneresa

Printed in the United States of America.
010053S17

TABLE OF CONTENTS

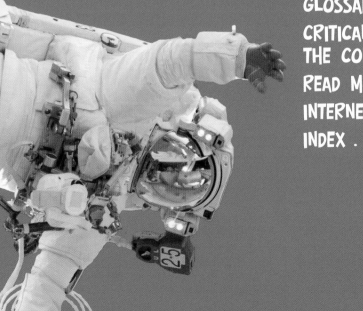

A YEAR IN SPACE

In March 2016 U.S. Astronaut Scott Kelly returned to Earth. He had lived in space for 340 days. During his stay on the International Space Station (ISS), Kelly performed many experiments. He also went on three spacewalks.

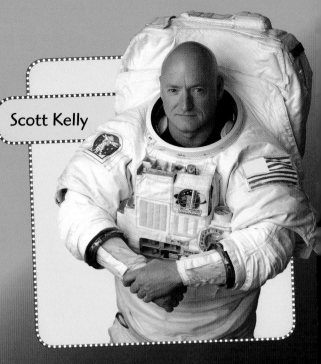

Scott Kelly

Scott Kelly on a spacewalk

Living in space is not easy. Astronauts are far from their families. And space can be dangerous. But many brave astronauts and cosmonauts have chosen to go there.

Kelly broke the U.S. record for the longest single mission in space. But this is not the world record. A cosmonaut named Valeri Polyakov lived in space longer. He spent 437 days, more than a year, on the Russian space station Mir. Mir was in space from 1986 to 2001.

SCOTT KELLY'S MISSION

2015

Launch

January
February
March

April
May
June

July
August
September

October
November
December

2016

Landing

January
February
March

April
May
June

July
August
September

October
November
December

THE FIRST SPACE STATION

Kelly spent his time in space at the ISS. More than 200 people have traveled to the ISS. It is the largest space station ever built. However it was not the first.

Salyut 1

A Soviet spacecraft docks with Salyut 1, the first space station.

The former Soviet Union launched a space station called Salyut 1 in 1971. Three cosmonauts lived there for 23 days. They tested equipment and performed experiments.

the crew that worked aboard Salyut 1

Space stations allow people to live in space for months at a time. They have large supplies of food, water, and air. A space station has more room inside to move around than a spacecraft does.

THE INTERNATIONAL SPACE STATION

The United States and Russia worked together to build the ISS. Other countries helped too. The first pieces, or modules, launched in 1998. The ISS is now the size of a football field.

Up to six people live on the ISS at one time. Their missions usually last six months.

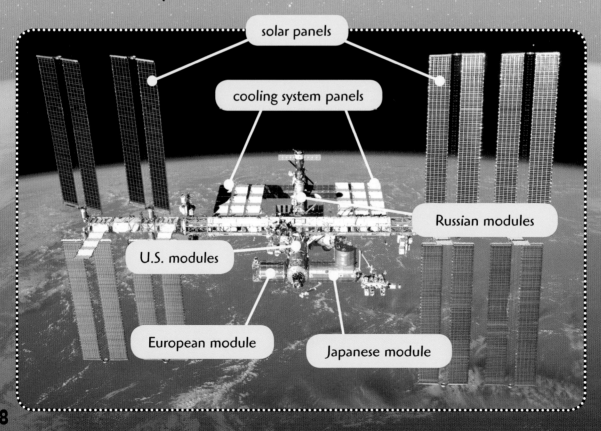

solar panels

cooling system panels

Russian modules

U.S. modules

European module

Japanese module

People from many nations have visited the ISS. The first British astronaut to fly for the European Space Agency (ESA) was Tim Peake. He lived on the ISS from late 2015 to early 2016.

TRAINING TO LIVE IN SPACE

Before astronauts live at the ISS, they need training. This takes up to two years. Astronauts learn how to work in space. They practice what to do in an emergency.

The U.S. astronauts use a full-sized model of the ISS for training. This model is in Houston, Texas. The astronauts spend months learning about the station's many systems.

Astronauts and instructors sit outside a model of the ISS and go over its systems.

ISS POWER TOOL

PART NUMBER 6E1557000
SERIAL NUMBER 002EU

German Astronaut Alexander Gerst trains for a spacewalk while hanging from wires.

GETTING TO THE ISS

Astronauts travel to the ISS in a Russian Soyuz capsule. Soyuz holds just three people. A rocket launches the capsule into space. About two days later, Soyuz docks with the ISS.

A rocket blasts a Soyuz capsule into space in 2012.

Soyuz capsule

250 miles
(400 kilometers)

9 minutes

SOYUZ LAUNCH

Rockets must travel upward to get into space. But they use most of
their energy to pick up speed when flying sideways. This lets them
stay in orbit, rather than falling back to Earth. A rocket has to push a
spacecraft up to more than 17,000 miles (27,400 kilometers) per hour
to reach the ISS. It takes a rocket about nine minutes to reach this
speed. By this time it is at a height of 250 miles (400 km).

WHAT TO WEAR

Astronauts wear heavy space suits and helmets during launch. This keeps them safe in case the spacecraft leaks air. Once they reach the ISS, they wear regular clothes.

The ISS has no washing machine. Work clothes are changed about every ten days. Socks and underwear are changed every other day.

Astronauts wear special space suits during spacewalks. These suits hold air and water. They keep astronauts at a comfortable temperature. They protect astronauts from the space environment. A space suit is a personal spacecraft.

EATING IN SPACE

An astronaut's food comes in different forms. Most food is dried. It is mixed with water before eating.

Earlier astronauts had food packaged in small tubes. Everything was blended into liquid. Astronauts ate through straws. Today's astronauts eat from other kinds of containers, including cans.

Tortillas are popular on the ISS. They are easy to store. They make fewer crumbs than bread. Crumbs could float away and get stuck in equipment.

AN ISS MENU

MEAL 1
- cottage cheese with nuts
- plum-cherry dessert
- cookies
- tea

MEAL 2
- seasoned scrambled eggs
- sausage patty
- oatmeal with raisins & spices
- waffle
- orange-grapefruit drink
- coffee

MEAL 3
- vegetable soup
- chicken with rice
- Moscow rye bread
- apple-peach juice

MEAL 4
- turkey
- tomatoes & eggplant
- shortbread cookies
- fruit cocktail
- tropical punch

DAILY LIFE IN SPACE

Each crew member has a small space about the size of a closet for sleeping. They attach a sleeping bag to the wall. That way they do not float around at night.

Using the bathroom in space is not easy. Astronauts first strap themselves to the toilets. This stops them from floating away. Then vacuums suck away waste.

sleeping bag

a toilet on the ISS

STAYING CLEAN

Every astronaut has a personal hygiene kit. Each kit includes toothpaste, a toothbrush, a comb, and other items. Astronauts brush their teeth twice a day. To save water, they do not rinse. Some swallow the toothpaste. Others spit into towels.

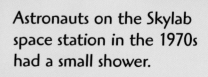

Astronauts on the Skylab space station in the 1970s had a small shower.

Today's astronauts use no-rinse shampoos on their hair. Using a towel, an astronaut rubs the liquid into her scalp. She uses another towel to wipe her head clean.

WORKING ON THE STATION

Astronauts spend much of their time working. Some watch how animals behave on the station. Others study plant growth in space. They also test how the body reacts to weightlessness.

Astronauts go on spacewalks to fix equipment outside the station. They repair or replace broken parts. Inside, they clean the walls and windows. Trash is collected and sent back toward Earth. It burns up as it travels through the atmosphere.

an astronaut on a spacewalk

EXPERIMENT	DESCRIPTION
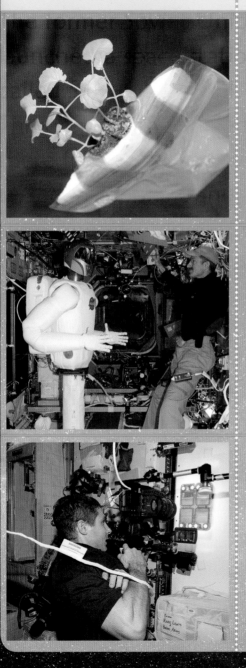	Astronauts grew plants from seeds on the ISS. The experiments showed how weightlessness, radiation, and light in the space station affect plant growth.
	Astronauts tested a robot called Robonaut on the ISS. In the future, robots will continue to help people do work both inside and outside the station.
	Astronauts used cameras to watch how ant behavior changed in weightlessness. Like ants, some robots move in swarms. Studying the way ants move and organize themselves may help scientists develop swarms of robots in the future.

RELAXING IN SPACE

Astronauts have some time to relax. They read books and watch movies. Astronauts read emails on computers or tablets. They also video chat with their families.

Another favorite pastime is simply looking out the window. Astronauts can watch lightning and hurricanes on Earth. They can see 16 sunsets every day.

Astronauts on the ISS watch a soccer game.

NEW YORK CITY IN THE UNITED STATES

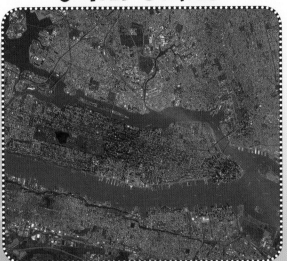

GOBI DESERT IN ASIA

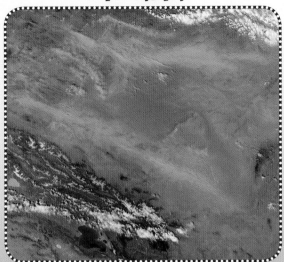

VOLCANO IN THE PACIFIC OCEAN

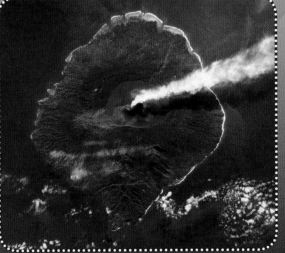

NEW ZEALAND

BODY CHANGES IN SPACE

Living in space is hard on the body. Gravity does not push against muscles and bones. They weaken. The heart also gets weaker. Because gravity is not pulling blood down, the heart does not have to pump as hard.

Floating in space is fun, but it can weaken the body.

To stay strong, astronauts exercise up to two hours each day. The ISS has a specially designed treadmill and bicycle. Astronauts attach themselves to the machines so they do not float away.

Astronaut Sunita Williams ran a marathon in space in 2007.

RETURNING TO EARTH

When astronauts are ready to come home, they board a Soyuz capsule. Parachutes slow down the capsule as it falls. Just before hitting the ground, small rockets fire. They slow the Soyuz for landing.

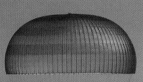

Right now living in space is limited to the ISS. But people may one day live on another planet. Astronauts may live on Mars for months or years. They will use the lessons learned on the ISS.

Mars

"[A] lot we have learned here from operating a space station will help us go to Mars. . . . anything we have ever put our mind to we have been able to accomplish."
—Scott Kelly, NASA astronaut

GLOSSARY

atmosphere—the air that surrounds Earth

capsule—a spacecraft that holds people

cosmonaut—a Russian astronaut

dock—to connect with another spacecraft in space

experiment—a scientific test

gravity—the force that pulls objects toward the center of Earth

hygiene—used to keep someone or something clean and healthy

model—something that is made to look like a person, animal, or object

module—an individual part of a space station

orbit—a path around an object, usually a star or planet, in space

spacewalk—leaving a spacecraft or space station to work outside

weightlessness—the feeling of not being pulled down toward Earth

CRITICAL THINKING USING THE COMMON CORE

1. Astronauts must exercise while they are living in space. Why is it important for them to exercise? (Key Ideas and Details)

2. What are the ways in which daily life in space is different from life on Earth? Are there any ways in which it is similar? (Integration of Knowledge and Ideas)

3. Turn to pages 16 and 17. How do these descriptions make you feel about space food? Would you like to eat in space? (Craft and Structure)

READ MORE

Bredeson, Carmen, and Marianne Dyson. *Astronauts Explore the Galaxy.* Launch into Space! New York: Enslow Publishing, 2015.

Buckley, James, Jr. *Home Address: ISS.* New York: Penguin Young Readers, 2015.

Hayden, Kate. *Astronaut: Living in Space.* New York: DK Publishing, 2012.

INTERNET SITES

FactHound offers a safe, fun way to find Internet sites related to this book. All of the sites on FactHound have been researched by our staff.

Here's all you do:

Visit www.facthound.com

Type in this code: 9781515736578

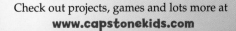

Super-cool stuff! Check out projects, games and lots more at **www.capstonekids.com**

INDEX